LET'S BEGIN!

GUIDE TO YOUR BEST SELF

Writing helps you to....

- Make sense of things that happened. When you write, you should describe all the details of the event as if you are speaking to someone who wasn't there. Be as descriptive as possible. Just the act of writing down the details of what happened may give you a new perspective of the situation or thought pattern.

- Speculate why something is the way it is. Your current views are a mixture of what you have heard from friends and family, things you have heard at a lecture or ideas you have read in a book. Either way, speculating why something is the way it is can be a very useful exercise in reasoning.

- Align your current thoughts and allow you to see if any changes are needed. Self reflection is key to growth!

- To get thoughts and ideas out of your head. Writing down your thoughts can help you relieve pressure and help resolve problems.

- To share your thoughts and ideas with others. Getting opinions from others about what you wrote can help you clarify your feelings for a deeper understanding of yourself.

Journal Writing Exercise

Tips to get started

1. Always keep your journal nearby

2. Write in your journal regularly

3. Get all of your thoughts and feelings out of your head and on paper

4. Review regularly

I AM ENOUGH.

THERE IS NO ONE BETTER TO BE THAN MYSELF.

Journal Writing

FEARLESS GEMS

1. What would you like to do this year that you have never done before?

_____
_____
_____
_____
_____
_____
_____
_____
_____
_____
_____
_____

Journal Writing

FEARLESS GEMS

2. List your areas of opportunity aka your weaknesses.

___
___
___
___
___
___
___
___
___
___
___

Journal Writing

FEARLESS GEMS

3. Imagine your life in 10 years. What does it look like? Let your mind run wild!

_____
_____
_____
_____
_____
_____
_____
_____
_____
_____
_____
_____
_____

Journal Writing

FEARLESS GEMS

4. List your strengths

Journal Writing

FEARLESS GEMS

5. Did anything make you feel hopeful today?

_____
_____
_____
_____
_____
_____
_____
_____
_____
_____
_____
_____

Journal Writing

FEARLESS GEMS

6. What is your interpretation of one of your recent dreams?

_____
_____
_____
_____
_____
_____
_____
_____
_____
_____
_____
_____

Journal Writing

FEARLESS GEMS

7. What part of your life could use some improvement?

_____
_____
_____
_____
_____
_____
_____
_____
_____
_____
_____
_____

Journal Writing

FEARLESS GEMS

8. When was the last time you did something for the first time? What did you do?

_____
_____
_____
_____
_____
_____
_____
_____
_____
_____
_____
_____
_____

Journal Writing

FEARLESS GEMS

9. Are you happy with yourself? Think about the inside and outside. Don't be afraid to get real!

_____
_____
_____
_____
_____
_____
_____
_____
_____
_____
_____

Journal Writing

FEARLESS GEMS

10. Describe who you would like to be when you are an adult.

_____
_____
_____
_____
_____
_____
_____
_____
_____
_____
_____
_____

Journal Writing

FEARLESS GEMS

11. Now that you have an idea of who you would like to be as an adult, what steps do you need to take to get there?

_____
_____
_____
_____
_____
_____
_____
_____
_____
_____
_____
_____
_____

Journal Writing

FEARLESS GEMS

12. What are your values? What are the things that are most important to you?
Ex: family

_____
_____
_____
_____
_____
_____
_____
_____
_____
_____
_____

Journal Writing

FEARLESS GEMS

13. What is your biggest goal? Is there anything stopping you from meeting this goal?

_____
_____
_____
_____
_____
_____
_____
_____
_____
_____
_____
_____
_____

Journal Writing

FEARLESS GEMS

14. How do you feel about how women are portrayed in media?

_____
_____
_____
_____
_____
_____
_____
_____
_____
_____
_____
_____

Journal Writing

FEARLESS GEMS

15. Do you think that the portrayal of women in media affects how people treat you?

_____
_____
_____
_____
_____
_____
_____
_____
_____
_____
_____

Journal Writing

FEARLESS GEMS

16. Do you use your time wisely? How can you do better?

_____
_____
_____
_____
_____
_____
_____
_____
_____
_____

Journal Writing

FEARLESS GEMS

17. What is your ideal home life like?

_____
_____
_____
_____
_____
_____
_____
_____
_____
_____
_____
_____

Journal Writing

FEARLESS GEMS

18. What can you do to make your home life more positive?

_____
_____
_____
_____
_____
_____
_____
_____
_____
_____
_____
_____

Journal Writing

FEARLESS GEMS

19. What are you most passionate about?

_____
_____
_____
_____
_____
_____
_____
_____
_____
_____
_____
_____
_____

Journal Writing

FEARLESS GEMS

20. What achievement are you most proud of? What will you do to top that one?

___
___
___
___
___
___
___
___
___
___
___

Journal Writing

FEARLESS GEMS

21. Describe yourself. Personality, aspirations, your beauty, likes, and dislikes.

_____
_____
_____
_____
_____
_____
_____
_____
_____
_____
_____
_____
_____
_____

Journal Writing

FEARLESS GEMS

22. What are the top 10 most important things in your life? Can money buy these?

Journal Writing

FEARLESS GEMS

23. What do you like most about yourself?

Journal Writing

FEARLESS GEMS

24. Do you love yourself? Why?

Journal Writing

FEARLESS GEMS

25. Is there something about yourself that you don't love?

_____
_____
_____
_____
_____
_____
_____
_____
_____
_____
_____
_____
_____

Journal Writing

FEARLESS GEMS

26. What are your biggest goals and dreams?

___
___
___
___
___
___
___
___
___
___
___

Journal Writing

FEARLESS GEMS

27. How will you learn to love that unique characteristic that you don't like?

_____
_____
_____
_____
_____
_____
_____
_____
_____
_____
_____
_____

Journal Writing

FEARLESS GEMS

28. Do you see yourself as a leader?

_____
_____
_____
_____
_____
_____
_____
_____
_____
_____
_____

Journal Writing

FEARLESS GEMS

29. What career field would you like to go into?

___
___
___
___
___
___
___
___
___
___
___

Journal Writing

FEARLESS GEMS

30. What would you do with 1 million dollars?

Journal Writing

FEARLESS GEMS

31. What makes you different from the other men and women in the career field you are thinking about pursuing?

_____
_____
_____
_____
_____
_____
_____
_____
_____
_____
_____
_____
_____
_____

TODAY I CHOOSE CONFIDENCE.

I CAN GET THROUGH ANYTHING.

Journal Writing

FEARLESS GEMS

32. What can you do to cope with a negative home life?

_____
_____
_____
_____
_____
_____
_____
_____
_____
_____
_____

Journal Writing

FEARLESS GEMS

33. Are you putting enough effort into your relationships?

Journal Writing

FEARLESS GEMS

34. What do you want to say to your future self?

_____
_____
_____
_____
_____
_____
_____
_____
_____
_____
_____
_____

Journal Writing

FEARLESS GE,MS

35. Am I letting matters that are out of my control stress me out?

_____
_____
_____
_____
_____
_____
_____
_____
_____
_____
_____
_____

Journal Writing

FEARLESS GEMS

36. Look back on today. What struck you most strongly?

_____
_____
_____
_____
_____
_____
_____
_____
_____
_____
_____
_____

Journal Writing

FEARLESS GEMS

37. Am I taking care of myself physically? Am I eating foods that properly fuel my body? Am I active enough?

Journal Writing

FEARLESS GEMS

38. Are you living true to yourself?

_____
_____
_____
_____
_____
_____
_____
_____
_____
_____
_____
_____

Journal Writing

FEARLESS GEMS

39. What do you find most frustrating?

_____
_____
_____
_____
_____
_____
_____
_____
_____
_____
_____

Journal Writing

FEARLESS GEMS

40. What would you do if you knew you could not fail?

_____
_____
_____
_____
_____
_____
_____
_____
_____
_____
_____
_____

Journal Writing

FEARLESS GEMS

41. Are you taking anything for granted?

___
___
___
___
___
___
___
___
___
___
___
___
___

Journal Writing

FEARLESS GEMS

42. What do you have to do to start achieving your ideal life?

_____
_____
_____
_____
_____
_____
_____
_____
_____
_____

Journal Writing

FEARLESS GEMS

43. What do you like to do in your free time?

_____
_____
_____
_____
_____
_____
_____
_____
_____
_____
_____
_____

Journal Writing

FEARLESS GEMS

44. What is your biggest fear?

_____
_____
_____
_____
_____
_____
_____
_____
_____
_____
_____
_____

Journal Writing

FEARLESS GEMS

45. Do you think that you can face your biggest fear alone or do you need someone with you?

_____
_____
_____
_____
_____
_____
_____
_____
_____
_____
_____
_____

Journal Writing

FEARLESS GEMS

46. Who are you? Really???

_____
_____
_____
_____
_____
_____
_____
_____
_____
_____
_____
_____

Journal Writing

FEARLESS GEMS

47. What are you running away from?

_____
_____
_____
_____
_____
_____
_____
_____
_____
_____
_____
_____
_____
_____

Journal Writing

FEARLESS GEMS

48. Are you settling for less than you are worth?

_____
_____
_____
_____
_____
_____
_____
_____
_____
_____
_____
_____

Journal Writing

FEARLESS GEMS

49. Listen to the voice inside your head. What has it told you today?

_____
_____
_____
_____
_____
_____
_____
_____
_____
_____
_____
_____

Journal Writing

FEARLESS GEMS

50. What positive things have you told yourself today?

_____
_____
_____
_____
_____
_____
_____
_____
_____
_____
_____
_____

Journal Writing

FEARLESS GEMS

51. What empowering belief can you start holding onto?

_____
_____
_____
_____
_____
_____
_____
_____
_____
_____
_____

Journal Writing

FEARLESS GEMS

52. What bad habits would you like to break?

_____
_____
_____
_____
_____
_____
_____
_____
_____
_____
_____
_____

Journal Writing

FEARLESS GEMS

53. Which one of your good habits would you like to cultivate?

_____
_____
_____
_____
_____
_____
_____
_____
_____
_____
_____

Journal Writing

FEARLESS GEMS

54. What is the meaning of life?

_____
_____
_____
_____
_____
_____
_____
_____
_____
_____
_____
_____

Journal Writing

FEARLESS GEMS

55. Do you find your mind traveling to the past or future more?

_____
_____
_____
_____
_____
_____
_____
_____
_____
_____

Journal Writing

FEARLESS GEMS

56. What is your purpose? Why do you exist?

_____
_____
_____
_____
_____
_____
_____
_____
_____
_____
_____
_____

Journal Writing

FEARLESS GEMS

57. What are you doing everyday to work towards your purpose (your reason for existing)?

_____
_____
_____
_____
_____
_____
_____
_____
_____
_____

Journal Writing

FEARLESS GEMS

58. Is there anything you can do to make your life more meaningful?

_____
_____
_____
_____
_____
_____
_____
_____
_____
_____
_____

Journal Writing

FEARLESS GEMS

59. What/who inspires you?

_____
_____
_____
_____
_____
_____
_____
_____
_____
_____
_____
_____
_____

Journal Writing

FEARLESS GEMS

60. You are like the 5 people you spend the most time with. Who does that include? Do you have good influences?

_____
_____
_____
_____
_____
_____
_____
_____
_____
_____
_____

Journal Writing

FEARLESS GEMS

61. Evaluate your circle of friends. Is there anyone in your circle that you do not want to be like?

_____
_____
_____
_____
_____
_____
_____
_____
_____
_____
_____
_____

Journal Writing

FEARLESS GEMS

62. What kind of trophy would you like to win?

_____
_____
_____
_____
_____
_____
_____
_____
_____
_____
_____
_____

Journal Writing

FEARLESS GEMS

63. Free write! What is on your mind?

_____
_____
_____
_____
_____
_____
_____
_____
_____
_____
_____
_____
_____

I MATTER.

I AM CAPABLE OF SO MUCH.

Journal Writing

FEARLESS GEMS

64. What is your ideal friend like? How does this ideal image compare to your actual friends?

___
___
___
___
___
___
___
___
___
___
___
___

Journal Writing

FEARLESS GEMS

65.. Are you afraid of letting people get close to you?

___
___
___
___
___
___
___
___
___
___
___

Journal Writing

FEARLESS GEMS

66. Think of the first person that hurt you. What did they do?

___
___
___
___
___
___
___
___
___
___
___

Journal Writing

FEARLESS GEMS

67. Are you making new people in your life pay for the mistakes that past people have made?

_____
_____
_____
_____
_____
_____
_____
_____
_____
_____
_____

Journal Writing

FEARLESS GEMS

68. Do you think you can completely heal from someone treating you wrong or seriously hurting your feelings?

_____
_____
_____
_____
_____
_____
_____
_____
_____
_____
_____
_____
_____

Journal Writing

FEARLESS GEMS

69. Do you think you can stop punishing innocent people from what someone in your past did?

___
___
___
___
___
___
___
___
___
___
___
___
___

Journal Writing

FEARLESS GEMS

70. Write a letter to yourself forgiving the person that hurt you the most. Forgiving them will release your pain!

_____
_____
_____
_____
_____
_____
_____
_____
_____
_____
_____
_____
_____

Journal Writing

FEARLESS GEMS

71. What is something that you have learned so far this year?

_____
_____
_____
_____
_____
_____
_____
_____
_____
_____
_____
_____

Journal Writing

FEARLESS GEMS

72. When did I last push the boundaries of my comfort zone?

_____
_____
_____
_____
_____
_____
_____
_____
_____
_____
_____
_____

Journal Writing

FEARLESS GEMS

73. Who is the most important person in the world to you? Why?

_____
_____
_____
_____
_____
_____
_____
_____
_____
_____

Journal Writing

FEARLESS GEMS

74. Do you have a mentor? Do you think you can benefit from one?

_____
_____
_____
_____
_____
_____
_____
_____
_____
_____
_____
_____
_____

Journal Writing

FEARLESS GEMS

75. What is something that you haven't told anyone?

_____
_____
_____
_____
_____
_____
_____
_____
_____
_____
_____
_____
_____
_____
_____

Journal Writing

FEARLESS GEMS

76. Free write! What's on your mind?

_____
_____
_____
_____
_____
_____
_____
_____
_____
_____
_____
_____

Journal Writing

FEARLESS GEMS

77. Do you have high or low self esteem? Why? What do you think causes low self-esteem in other people?

Journal Writing

FEARLESS GEMS

78. Do you like the person that you are becoming? What would you like to change?

_____
_____
_____
_____
_____
_____
_____
_____
_____
_____
_____
_____

Journal Writing

FEARLESS GEMS

79. How is your relationship with your parents?

_____
_____
_____
_____
_____
_____
_____
_____
_____
_____
_____
_____

Journal Writing

FEARLESS GEMS

80. What can you do to help your community?

_____
_____
_____
_____
_____
_____
_____
_____
_____
_____
_____
_____

Journal Writing

FEARLESS GEMS

81. Do you have anyone that just "gets you"? How is your relationship with them?

_____
_____
_____
_____
_____
_____
_____
_____
_____
_____
_____
_____
_____

I AM AN AWESOME LEADER.

EVERYDAY IS A FRESH START.

Journal Writing

FEARLESS GEMS

82. What is something that you are curious about? Look it up!

_____
_____
_____
_____
_____
_____
_____
_____
_____
_____
_____
_____

Journal Writing

FEARLESS GEMS

83. Have you made any progress with the goal you made this year?

___
___
___
___
___
___
___
___
___
___
___
___

Journal Writing

FEARLESS GEMS

84. Lets talk about your choices when it comes to your body! Do you feel like you make good choices when it comes to your health?

Journal Writing

FEARLESS GEMS

85. Do you fit your idea of beauty? If not, what needs to change; your beauty or your idea of beauty?

___
___
___
___
___
___
___
___
___
___
___
___
___
___

Journal Writing

FEARLESS GEMS

THE END! 85 questions, wow what source of inspiration. Journaling is used to capture all your reflections, you will eventually get a better picture of your thoughts and feelings towards different areas in your life.

This was a special project created by Ms. Kris and Ms. Penny the co-founders, dedicated to all of our gems.

Check us out at Gemnme.com

Made in the USA
Monee, IL
24 September 2021